Why Polar Bears Like Snow... and Flamingos Don't

BY NANCY WHITE

Table of Contents

CHAPTER 1

Different Places, Different Animals

Different kinds of animals live in different kinds of places. For example, polar bears live in the freezing cold Arctic. You would never see one in the South American rain forest. Flamingos wade around in swampy **wetlands**. They are never seen bounding across the African grasslands. The special kind of place where an animal lives is called the animal's **habitat.**

polar bear

flamingo

The polar bear's thick, heavy fur is just right for keeping out the Arctic cold. The flamingo's long, skinny legs are perfect for wading in swamps and marshes. These animals are just right for the habitats in which they live. Being just right for a habitat is called being **adapted.**

Turn the page to visit habitats all over the world. Find out about the amazing ways animals are adapted to their habitats.

The Arctic: It's Cold Out There!

Arctic

The **Arctic,** way up near the North Pole, is very cold. The ground is covered with snow almost all year long. There are not very many trees or plants. In the summer the Sun never really sets, but in fall and winter, it is dark most of the time. The temperature in winter is usually about -30° Fahrenheit (-34° Celsius), and it can get even colder. Arctic animals are adapted for life in a cold place. They have some interesting ways of keeping warm and protecting themselves.

One way Arctic animals stay warm is by having lots of fur. Another is by having a lot of fat. Polar bears have both: lots of warm fur and a thick layer of fat just under the skin. The fat acts like an extra layer of clothing to keep out the cold.

Seals and walruses have a thick layer of fat, too. It is called **blubber**. The thick layer of blubber under their skins keeps them warm, even in the freezing waters of the Arctic Ocean.

Meet the Walrus

Size: Up to 12 feet long

Weight: Up to 3,000 pounds

Life Span: Up to 40 years

Favorite Food: Shellfish

Main Enemy: The polar bear

Interesting Fact: The walrus' tusks are really very long teeth. A walrus uses its tusks to defend itself and as hooks when climbing out of the water onto ice.

Arctic hare

jackrabbit

Believe it or not, having small ears helps keep an animal warm. A lot of the warmth from an animal's body escapes through the ears. Arctic animals need to keep in all the body heat they can. The Arctic hare has smaller ears than most rabbits. And the Arctic fox's ears are smaller than those of foxes that live in warmer habitats.

Many of the animals living in the Arctic are white. They are hard to see because they blend in with the white snow. Coloring that makes an animal blend in with its surroundings is called **camouflage**.

Camouflage protects the white Arctic hare from other animals that might hunt and kill it for food. Camouflage helps animals that hunt, too. The white polar bear can creep over the snow and ice and never be seen by the seals it hunts and eats.

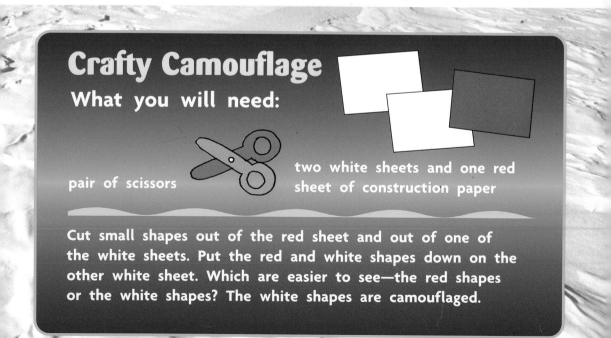

Crafty Camouflage

What you will need:

pair of scissors

two white sheets and one red sheet of construction paper

Cut small shapes out of the red sheet and out of one of the white sheets. Put the red and white shapes down on the other white sheet. Which are easier to see—the red shapes or the white shapes? The white shapes are camouflaged.

Question:

How does changing color help the Arctic fox survive?

The Arctic fox and the Arctic hare actually change color. In the summer, when the snow melts, they shed their white fur and grow a grayish coat. When the snow comes back, their white fur grows back again!

This is an Arctic fox in the winter.

This is an Arctic fox in the summer.

The Tropical Rain Forest of South America: Hot and Humid

Tropical rain forests are found near the, equator. It is very hot and damp there, and there are lots of tall trees.

tropical rain forest

The tropical rain forest is really like three habitats in one. The canopy is the highest level, up in the treetops. The understory is the middle level, lower down in the trees. The forest floor is the lowest level, down on the ground. Different animals live at each level.

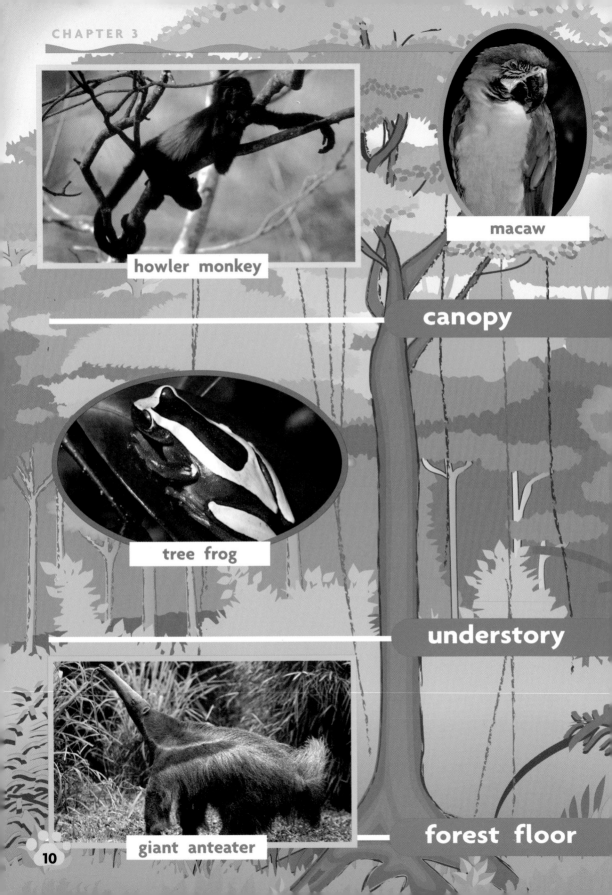

howler monkey

macaw

canopy

tree frog

understory

giant anteater

forest floor

Most of the animals of the canopy never come down to the ground. They are adapted to their high habitat because they can fly or climb trees. Some of the flying animals are colorful insects and birds.

Monkeys are the great tree climbers of the canopy. They can swing from one tree branch to another with their arms. Some monkeys can even wrap their tails around branches, using them as extra arms as they swing through the trees.

The tree frog has special sticky toes that help it climb trees. It can jump and capture insects as they fly by.

It's a FACT!

Did you know that the jaguar is the only big cat that doesn't roar?

The understory is home to many members of the cat family. They are excellent climbers and can easily jump from tree to tree. Some of these big cats have spots that make them hard to see in the shadowy branches.

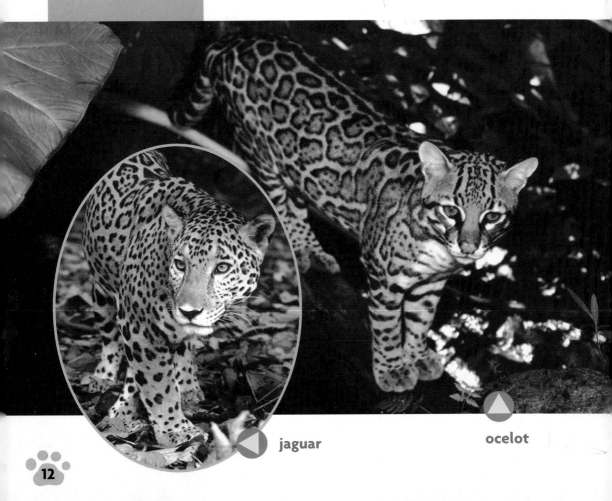

jaguar

ocelot

sloth

Meet the Kinkajou

The sloth spends most of its time hanging upside down from green, leafy branches in the understory. Because the sloth moves so slowly, it can't run away from other animals. It depends on camouflage to hide from its enemies. Tiny green plants called **algae** grow in the sloth's fur and make it look green!

Size: About three feet long, including its tail

Favorite Foods: Fruit and birds' eggs

Habits: Sleeps all day curled up in a hole in a tree. Rarely comes down to the ground.

Interesting Fact: Can hang from its tail...and then climb up it!

giant anteater

Some strange-looking animals live on the rain-forest floor. One of these is the giant anteater.

The giant anteater uses its long claws to dig into ants' nests. It has a long, skinny head that can poke into the narrow hole it digs. The anteater then catches the ants with its very long, sticky tongue.

The Grasslands of Africa: Wide Open Spaces

African grasslands

The African grasslands, also called **savannas,** are also near the equator. The African grasslands are very dry and covered with tall grass. The land is mostly flat, so you can see for a long distance in any direction. There are hardly any trees for animals to climb. There are no leaves or dark, shady places to hide in.

Question:

Why do you think it is dangerous for animals to be out in the open?

Meet the Ostrich

Size: Up to 8 feet tall—the world's largest bird

Weight: Up to 350 pounds. Each egg weighs 3 pounds!

Favorite Foods: Plants and grass

Speed: Can run 40 miles per hour, but can't fly.

Interesting Fact: Females sit on eggs in the daytime. Males sit on eggs at night.

Speed can be very important when there is no place to hide. Many grassland animals are fast runners. The cheetah, the world's fastest land animal, can run 70 miles per hour! Running fast helps an animal chase and catch other animals for food. Running fast also helps an animal get away when it is being chased.

cheetah

giraffe

Animals in the African grasslands are adapted to their habitat in other ways, too.

The giraffe has a very long neck for eating leaves from the tops of trees.

The tan lion is camouflaged in the light-brown grass. Hidden in the grass, it can sneak up on animals, such as zebras, that it hunts for food.

Notice how this lion blends into the golden-tan grasses of the savanna.

It's a FACT!

Just as small ears help some Arctic animals stay warm, big ears help some grassland animals, like the elephant, stay cool. Another grassland animal, the bat-eared fox, has much bigger ears than other foxes.

African elephant

bat-eared fox

red fox

Elephants are big and strong and travel in packs so most other animals do not attack them. Since they eat plants, they do not need to hunt other animals.

The Everglades of Florida: Water World

Everglades

Wetlands are swampy, marshy places where the ground is muddy and wet. One of the most famous wetlands in the world is a huge swamp in Florida called the Everglades.

Alligators, frogs, turtles, raccoons, snakes, many kinds of birds, and many kinds of insects live in the Everglades. All of them are adapted to a wet habitat where it's hard to walk or run.

Make a Chart

Copy this chart on a sheet of paper. Write down how you think each animal moves. (You may want to use an animal more than once on the chart.)

Animals: alligator, frog, turtle, raccoon, snake, bird, insect

Climb	Fly	Slither	Swim	Jump	Wade

Meet the Muskrat

Size: 1 foot long without tail; 10-inch-long tail.

Favorite Foods: Plants, fish, and shellfish

Habits: Spends most of its time in the water. Uses its flat tail to steer while swimming.

Home: Builds a "house" by plastering plants together with mud.

Interesting Facts: Has webbed toes on its hind feet. Has an unpleasant smell.

Some of the birds that live in the Everglades have very long legs. Their legs are so long, they can wade in water. Some of these birds can also fly.

white ibis

roseate spoonbill

Alligators are so well camouflaged that you have to look very hard to see them. An alligator can stay just beneath the surface of the water. Nothing shows above the surface except its eyes and its nostrils. If you did see an alligator floating in the water, you might think it was just a log. The alligator can breathe and see without being noticed by other animals.

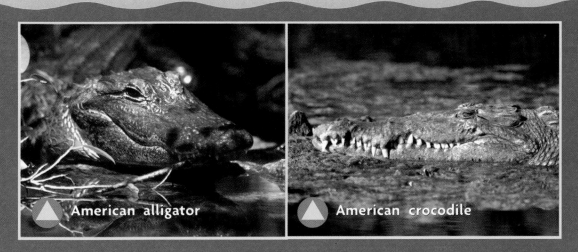

American alligator

American crocodile

Gators and Crocs

Do you know how to tell the difference between an alligator and a crocodile? When an American alligator has its mouth closed, you cannot see its lower teeth. When an American crocodile has its mouth closed, you can always see its lower teeth.

CHAPTER 6

Animals Around You

You've read about some amazing animals that live in different habitats. Now think about the habitat you live in. Is it hot? Is it very cold? Is it wet? Do you live in a city, suburb, or rural place? What kinds of animals live around you?

Look at the animals, and observe how they behave. Can you tell how they are adapted to their habitat?

Animal	How Is It Adapted?

Glossary

adapted	just right for an animal's *habitat*
algae	tiny green plants
Arctic	very cold *habitat* near the North Pole
blubber	layer of fat under an animal's skin
camouflage	coloring or other characteristics that make it hard to see an animal in its surroundings
canopy	the top level of the *tropical rain forest*
equator	an imaginary line around Earth that separates the Northern Hemisphere from the Southern Hemisphere
forest floor	the bottom level of the *tropical rain forest*
habitat	type of place where an animal lives
savannas	hot, dry *habitats* where there is tall grass and few trees
tropical rain forest	a hot, damp, tropical *habitat* with many trees
understory	the middle level of the *tropical rain forest*
wetlands	swampy, marshy *habitats*

Index